I0528963

Advance Praise for
This Tangled Body

In Carmen Calatayud's astounding collection *This Tangled Body*, surreal imagery and language cut and soar to make luminous a pain that is both individual and generational. Anyone who has missed—as I have—poetry born out of the grit of lived experience and transmuted into indelible lyric should buy this book at once. As a member of the same generation, I am moved and haunted by how acutely Calatayud captures our yearning and our restlessness, teaching us to love with renewed vigor our much-broken world. Calatayud writes, "I don't know peace but I know/how to speak under my breath./How to make noise." I am in love with every poem in this wild, original, and utterly necessary book.

—**Sheila Black**, author of *Radium Dream* and
editor of *Beauty is a Verb: The New Poetry of Disability*

"Life started as the time between wars/then became the wars themselves," writes Carmen Calatayud in *This Tangled Body*, a lyrical collection meditating on the body's internalization of perpetual global conflict. Living rooms are war zones created by parents "who survived war themselves" and intimates are enemy combatants that treat bodies as battlefields. As such, the poet's language oscillates between lustful and concussive, creating verse that lives in the pleasure-pain duality of the body's experience. Calatayud seeks to untangle herself from the stranglehold trauma has on the optimism and self-determined healing she is seeking. In essence, this collection reminds us that the only way to "Love as if today [is our] last day on the planet" is to love hard.

—**John Olivares Espinoza**, author of *The Date Fruit Elegies*

Let Carmen Calatayud's poetry guide you in uncovering what lies beyond the wall. With the Spanish Civil War, the Vietnam War, and conflicts in Central America as backdrops, it offers an intimate glimpse of the battle on the home front of our pathologies. This struggle includes literal and metaphorical body counts, and the cyclic torment of trying to flee the emotional front lines of our lives through addiction. Calatayud leads us to "negotiate with decades of despondency" while "welcoming all the beings of the broken world." Finally, we are compelled to admit the truth about our own secrets, even if it is only to ourselves.

—**Angelina Sáenz**, author of *Edgecliff* and *Maestra*

Open *This Tangled Body*, and you will find imagery like Lorca's that stuns you and takes you out of this world and into an expanding universe. Open this book and you will find a heart continually opening to encompass your own wounds. This collection straddles the spirit world and what we call the real world by taking us to the land of the dead with all its terrifying ghosts and then resuscitating us. From the first poem, we, too, believe in "the skeleton of a horse (that) runs along the wall." Calatayud steps compassionately over all borders to face a history of abuse and injustice—from a complicated family history to xenophobia to her own violated woman's body—to find healing. In these beautifully crafted poems, Calatayud faces destruction to rise from the ashes and ultimately find grace.

—**Pamela Uschuk**, author of *Crazy Love*,
winner of the American Book Award and
Refugee, a *Kirkus Review* top favorite book

This Tangled Body

FLOWERSONG
PRESS

poems by

Carmen Calatayud

FLOWERSONG
PRESS

FlowerSong Press
Copyright © 2024 by Carmen Calatayud
ISBN: 978-1-963245-59-2

Published by FlowerSong Press
in the United States of America.
www.flowersongpress.com

Set in Adobe Garamond Pro
Cover Image by Aydee Lopez Martinez
Cover Design by Priscilla Celina Suarez

This Tangled Body by Carmen Calatayud received a subvention from Letras Latinas, the literary initiative at the University of Notre Dame's Institute for Latino Studies—as part of its on-going effort to support Latinx poets and community-minded publishing.

No part of this book may be reproduced without
written permission from the Publisher.

All inquiries and permission requests should
be addressed to the Publisher.

NOTICE: SCHOOLS AND BUSINESSES
FlowerSong Press offers copies of this book at quantity discount with bulk purchase for educational, business, or sales promotional use. For information, please email the Publisher at info@flowersongpress.com.

For my parents, Juan Bautista Calatayud and Helen Lupton Calatayud,
who gave everything they had

Art by
Aydee Lopez Martinez

table of contents

II

III

IV

Introduction

You wonder how much a human soul can carry. What burden is too much? When does the soul break beyond repair? What does it mean to be broken? It's both terrifying and awe-inspiring to know what people are capable of surviving.

We talk a lot about the idea of healing but not about its particulars. Different people heal differently, unevenly, partially, and sometimes not at all. People can also heal wrong, the same way a bone can heal wrong and need to be re-broken and set correctly. But sometimes things can't be re-broken, and sometimes we can't bear to re-break them.

Carmen Calatayud's poetry in this collection spans all of those places—the wounded, the broken, the partially healed, and what is beyond healing. *This Tangled Body* is an illustration of surviving. Not every story concerned with wounds or healing can be about reaching the other shore. Sometimes a story needs to be about the value of treading water. Because to tread water is to survive. Treading water is not drowning. Treading water is to hold out hope for healing in the future.

Calatayud's work spans worlds of wounds. The wounds of inheriting war, witnessing and experiencing addiction and physical/sexual/psychological violence, a life framed by the repercussions of four concussions, a body that inherited pain and finds peace and rest elusive.

There will always be people who don't understand the necessity of poetry—the necessity of writing it or sharing it or reading it. But as the poet Levi Romero told me decades ago, for some of us no nos queda de otra. There is nothing else that can soothe us, nothing else that can make life bearable, nothing else that call fill us or lift us or know us. There is no other way.

Empathy has its limits. We can't ever wholly know another person's wounds or all the ways those wounds burned into the fissures and tissues of their beings. So then poetry like this arrives. Somehow finding its way into the world, focused like sunlight through a magnifying glass, speaking and burning, revealing and dissecting. Poetry that tells us stories we don't know, with as much honesty and directness as the poet can access. Even though the complete story remains elusive—because there are too many things that still can't be told.

We meet the narrator as a girl-woman: "She puts the needle down on an album and hears/'Happiness is a Warm Gun'/over and over/as she lies on the floor/ear to the speaker/to float away from the war zone/created by parents/who survived wars themselves."

Then the narrator as a woman who "pulls into parking lot at a grocery store/windshield absorbs her hyena sounds/It's springtime in April/she rolls down the windows/air/more/air/the dogwoods are in bloom." And we can't know—is the narrator poet more hurt by suffering or by the indifferent beauty of the blooming dogwoods?

The driving need to survive, to heal, is always there. An insistent drumbeat, directed inwards and outwards: "Me wanting you to want to/save yourself." As is the never-quenched need to release what we can release, to be forced to release what we don't want to release, and confronting the realities of what we can't release: "Pilar dies two days later. Kept comfortable as she labored to breathe./Holy Morphine. Magic Morphine. Mother of Morphine./Her bedside free of lifesaving machines./How we left behind refuse to let go./How we die too when we finally release."

Calatayud understands something that most of us won't accept. That there is a place for all the partially broken, all the wholly broken. She says, "My arms opened to wave them in, to welcome all the beings of the broken world."

—ire'ne lara silva

This Tangled Body

The things that women reclaim are often their own voice, their own values, their imagination, their clairvoyance, their stories, their ancient memories. If we go for the deeper, and the darker, and the less known, we will touch the bones.

—**Clarissa Pinkola Estés**

i put a butterfly on my tongue
a music serenading the night
into stars, turning darkness
into a harvest of melody.

—**Taofeek Ayeyemi**

I

Walls

What I told you under the covers
is everything I believe.

The skeleton of a horse runs along the wall.

You must climb over walls to take your place.
Those in charge, if you wait for them
to do the right thing,
you'll be waiting 17 lifetimes.

Listen to the bones in a galloping horse.

Don't awaken to a day that has already
been written and pretend to hope.
The right thing won't come to you.
You have to take it.

Years fall off the calendar of a horse's frame.

There are walls everywhere.
Your work is to knock them down with your eyes.
Then go toward tenderness.

Horse is your ancestor.
Ancestors never disappear when you are conjuring a life.

What I told you under the covers
is everything I believe.

Godmother

There's a woman on her front porch
Inhaling her cigarette. She's in love

With the slender white stick
Between her fingers.

My fingers pretend to play piano
While tapping my left arm.

Blue-green vein rises and
I stroke it like a purring cat.

It's been four weeks, heroin,
And I need you to feel nothing.

There is so much I want to tell you—
I want to thank you for being my godmother

For taking me to the church where god doesn't care
And we don't pretend he does.

Truth blooms in a way a moon girl can understand
Truth being there is no me.

Just velvet junk afterglow that
Streams from stars into my arm.

Wish magic alone could blow my heart open
Fill it with a mouth to kiss all the losses.

On the sidewalk in front of my feet
A grey feather just landed.

The woman lights another cigarette
The smoke smells like her name, Dulce.

I pick up the feather and put its point
To my vein, dream of burnt caramel

Streaming in, lips smack from fast joy—
The sweet blur gone too quick.

Death Bed

In my job as a grief counselor at a hospice,
I'm called on to visit a Spanish-speaking patient.
I visit Pilar at her bedside.

Young, in her 40s.
Fuzzy hair regrowth after chemo.
She is tiny, with shriveled features of a gamine.

Pilar is dying in the same bed where my father died six years before.
I speak to her in Spanish, gently touch her wasted arm
in the hope that skin-to-skin contact will soothe her.

As she sleeps with an IV morphine drip connected to her vein,
I'm on her right side, and remember that as my father lay comatose
I sat on his left.

I walk over to the left side of the bed,
as though sitting in that same spot
might conjure my father. The man who
I forgave at his bedside hours before he died
only because my friend Rosie convinced me to.
To give respite to him. To me.

/

Pilar. Pilar. Pilar.

Is it possible to conjure a spirit who won't allow

this mother of two children to leave her body?
I rock my hips, willing her to survive, even though she's in a hospice bed.

Pilar dies two days later. Kept comfortable as she labored to breathe.
Holy Morphine. Magic Morphine. Mother of Morphine.
Her bedside free of lifesaving machines.

How we left behind refuse to let go.
How we die too when we finally release.

First Concussion

Large crystal ashtray at center of scene:

Girl, 17, lying on couch

Boy, 16, grabs ashtray with right hand

uses left hand to squeeze her neck

push it into rust-colored cushion

thrusts the weight on top of her head

blow   blow   blow blow blow

to the skull

stack of breath stuck in her windpipe

When finished he bangs ashtray

back on the coffee table where it lives

Girl chokes   screams like a strangled swan

                          tongue sputters

                                  touches her head

                           finds three lumps rising

feels loose teeth inside her mouth

                     Words broken

                                  wails unattended

FM radio still on in her room

                      a song from the 70's she is sick of hearing

grabs car keys

                       drives to nowhere

      steers

                     shakes

passes azalea bush full of pink

pulls into parking lot at a grocery store

windshield absorbs her hyena sounds

It's springtime in April

                she rolls down the windows

     air
           more
                          air

the dogwoods are in bloom

Post-War Hunger
Comunidad Valenciana, España (1939-1942)

Our dreams brown almonds.
Our eyes brown almonds.

This violet sky rains almonds.
I try to catch one on my tongue.

The rest drop to the ground and
We gather them in sacks for sustenance.

We stop to break open a few and eat together.

We kneel because generations
Gave love to these native trees.

The tree limbs grew to the clouds, and
The clouds released almonds.

We smuggle almonds in aprons and pants.
The wind is hungry so we feed it almonds.

We labyrinth our way home with hope inside our skulls.
Our DNA sings under the sun.

Today we don't taste blue emptiness.
We taste bark, branch and shell.

For tonight we are stripped of the tick-tock of fear.

Love in the Time of Sleeplessness

This might be a sleepless love poem

                              about wandering through wet fog

            where orange blossom scent bleeds into air

like a nick on the wrist that won't clot

      This might be a sleepless love poem

about the grief of melodic ghosts

                        who leave copper stains on the floor and

                              song lyrics inside walls

This might be a sleepless

                  love poem about resurrection between legs

                        flesh that remembers satellite touch and

steam that comes from a stray exhale

            This might be

a sleepless love poem

about my nostalgic heart and your monstrous hands

that were once an x-ray of improbable bones

This might be a sleepless
love poem

about how we can't find Eros

or Jupiter's trail, but we take a corner of the sky—

a part of it that goes unnoticed and

still hums

Watching the War, 1975

On April 29, 1975 and into the following morning, major American news networks reported that Operation Frequent Wind transported more than 1,000 Americans and more than 5,000 Vietnamese out of Saigon at the end of the Vietnam War.

Too hard to take her father's blows for talking during the news so after 8 pm,

                              she moves to her room
      slips into a narcotic haze.

               After more chugs of cherry cough medicine,

the empty bottle glows:

          Iridescent, a pale ruby cylinder.

      She cuts across her wrist horizontally three times

                with a rusty razor

         not knowing that vertical

is the way to go.

             Blood barely blossoms from her shy left wrist.

* * *

This girl is addicted to music that spins

on a spinach green record player from Sears.

She puts the needle down on an album and hears

"Happiness is a Warm Gun"
over and over

as she lies on the floor

ear to the speaker

to float away from the war zone

created by parents
who survived wars themselves.

* * *

On the news that night, she sees the Vietnamese
climb American embassy walls.

U.S. Marines slammed their gripping fingers with butts of guns

watched men and women fall.

The reporter said a Vietnamese government official left behind

shot himself to death.

* * *

The girl pretends she is airlifted to another place
by grabbing hold of a magic helicopter

ready to hang on like the Vietnamese people

who reached for the skids

of the last American chopper that took off in April '75

but were left behind: running, jumping, crying out.

* * *

She can't tell the difference between her body and

                bodies desperate to escape

                              across the screen.

          Reaches her hand into television land

   to bring refugees into her space.

* * *

Codeine makes the music rise like an aquamarine wave

                      and crash across her cheeks.

      Then Jimi Hendrix comes back to life

   to take her from this shell-shocked house

         to a place where everything's fluid and blue.

Jimi reels her into a kaleidoscope dream

              where there's a reunion with the dead
   as he sings "Castles Made of Sand."

Waterlogged

After Amirah Al Wassif

I had a dream that I was a catfish dancing at night.

Saturn escaped from the cosmos, dove into the Chesapeake Bay.

In that dream my dead husband rose

out of the water with a seaweed guitar.

I had a dream that my Gaelic mother was lying

near the Wild Atlantic Way. In that dream

I was a dolphin who nosed her back

into the ocean where she was born.

I had a dream that I was captain of a ship lost

on the floor of the sea. In that dream it took

living as an octopus with eight arms to

pull passengers out. I ached in the fog.

I had a dream that I was a drowning teenage boy

who pretended death was the route to kismet.

Who knew that oxygen was something to be savored—

that letting breath out of a bottle would show me how to rise.

Last Night in My Father's House

Moonlight spills through this window
      for the last time.

Such dignity, la luna.

She catches her breath, exhales an angel with shredded wings
      who cowers under my bed.
Even the angel of death who comes for my father
      is scared tonight.

II

Water Bottles at the Border

After *Desire Lines, Baboquivari Peak, AZ, 2004*
by Delilah Montoya

Dream: A saint with a white guayabera
Unloads jugs to dot the desert
Water to ease swelling tongues.

He walks for wandering people
Leaves bottles for thirsty women
In this burnt coral sunset land:
Two countries so close the border
Evaporates at night.

Filled plastic jugs hidden behind
Jumping cholla in this vista of hope.

Awake: The monsters of fire will come
For us, gun us down under
A moon of ginger flames
Just as our whispers begin to rise.

This borderland named many times
Stolen and taken back again.
The saguaros refuse to fight
Stretch into glitter-blue sky as
White heat feeds the ground.

We chant for survival.
Ravens fly overhead
Offer ebony rings of faith.

If no one knows us
Our bones will mingle
With this dry earth.
They will hiss our names
In the wind.

Refugee Couple

After the bombs we collected bones.
I found a femur.

But you are the spoils from all the wars,
the battles between tribes and broken nations.
Life started as the time between the wars,
then became the wars themselves.

The night we ate a blackbird and
prayed he wasn't sick.
Rancid bread,
all of the hushed quarter moons:
These memories of wartime.

I don't want to remember,
but then you remind me that we survived.
That we were able to hide in the closet and hum.

We lived through separate wars
but spoke the same language of dread.

I don't know peace but I know
how to speak under my breath.
How to make noise
in the brief times of safety.
In the crux of the ruptured world.

Never mind all that.
I love you from here
to the border and back again.

Let's leave this continent and
light the path behind us on fire.
Freedom is family you don't need any more.
I'll roll my heart into a sleeping bag and
wear it on my back.

We'll walk out of this place, far from secret police.
Kiss me before the sun reveals our shapes.
Before our shadows imprint the wall.

First Generation Daughter at the Shore

After Taofeek Ayeyemi

The ocean said it knew her
       but she didn't know herself.

No one's daughter, just a body of two cultures

          born into a third unnerving land
miles from Atlantic City.

A pink shell used as shelter
       for not belonging to her parents' countries

or to a nation that requires
       a permanent bulletproof vest.

There was living inside The Sea of Not Feeling.
       The Sea of Slowly Losing Her Fists.

Wrestling with swells of trouble,
       she searched for survival in waves.

How to untwine from paternal machismo rule
       and maternal conquested fear.

Breasts and ovaries were planted in the sand
       without permission.

Washed into water,
repeatedly forced back to shore.

Legs grew out of coral that floated north from the Keys.

Arms sprouted from torso pits.

She made her way with all of her parts to a bonfire of mad intentions—
sucked on wine

talked with a skeleton on the ocean floor

then learned to walk toward land
instead of waiting for bones to float
to the top of the foam.

Swollen Heart

I remember the animal craziness of our life:
Video porn, wet sex delirium on the living room floor,
banging the wooden loveseat frame
against a thin apartment wall—
Who cared if the neighbors complained?
Red tulip walks with too much sky
flying above the cemetery
in between days of espresso and beer
while you painted and I scribbled poems
to perch on your easel at night.
Our fertile hurricane.

You transmuted when you threw cobalt blue on canvas—
Your cadmium red and raven black paintings
allowed our nightmares to shine.
Those creations cradled me,
gave us permission to float
away from this wasted world.
We tried to speak for the almost dead
with body-part collages and bird skulls found,
my disease-filled lyrics for the music you wrote.

Just two months after we planned to meet again,
your blood splashed, left ventricle to right,
chambers decayed into glitter of death you envisioned
but not like this:
Swollen heart, fluid filled.
Me wishing I went with you bad enough

that driving drunk on grief caused me to crash.
I begged Saint Jude to bring you back,
pigeons to break through your ribs,
peck at your chest.
For pulses from your electric guitar to buzz your atrium,
save you from falling into astral blue dusk.
But the saint of lost causes didn't trick death or
morph you into a Lazarus.
On better days, I recite incantations to make me
want to stay in this world.
I fool myself while you watch.

Boy With No Name

When my son died
a thousand miles away
I made my arms a cradle.
                    —Kelle Groom

In the dream, it's wintertime and I hate winter. I'm scared of the cold in the dream as well as in real life because my body can never get warm enough.

There is a hill with a naked tree, its limbs shivering. There is snow and wind and a dead grey sky, with no hope that winter will ever end. I'm not sure I can survive if there's no escape from the cold.

Then a voice: *I know this is the winter of your discontent. I have not forsaken you.*

I wake up sobbing into my pillow even though there's bright desert sunlight streaming into this bedroom in Tucson. This voice, a mixture of Shakespeare and Jesus, is unlike anything I've ever heard in a dream. I'm convinced it was the voice of some higher power that hasn't forgotten me.

This dream comes one week before I learn the reason I've been feeling so sick for the past two months, much more than usual.

* * *

When I was the moon, I wasn't whole. Just a blue half-circle drifting through the sky. After I sloughed off pieces of myself I became a quarter moon, a sliver of light that gingerly rocked back and forth like a porch swing.

This is what I remember after the abortion—just a sliver of me being left, and a sliver of a child being sucked out of my uterus with a vacuum that hurt more than I could have imagined. It hurt so badly that I asked the doctor to stop. He couldn't. I got dizzy from the sharpness of the puncture and suction.

My son was sucked out of me and spit into the sky. I couldn't imagine where else he could go, so I saw his cells in the Sonoran Desert darkness.

Each small star was a spark of my boy, glitter above me every night.

*   *   *

I go to the doctor because I feel sick, more than I usually do from adrenal fatigue. Since the doctor is concerned about an ovarian cyst, she does a sonogram. I look at the screen as she drags the gel-covered wand back and forth across my skin, until a black and white picture appears.

"You're pregnant."

"Are you sure?" I'm stunned and feel my cheeks burn from the shame that I'm pregnant and didn't know it. I've been nauseous for weeks, and had missed my period, but my period was already erratic.

It's a few days before the 12-week cut off for legal abortions, so the doctor reminds me that I have to decide quickly.

"I'll support you whatever you decide," she reassures me, her voice steady, warm. Then she pauses and I hold my breath.

"But you need to know that this is going to be a difficult pregnancy."

I imagine what it would be like to hold my son. What he would look like, how he would sound. An August-born boy. I consider his father: A heavy drinker, cocaine user and gambler who insists he is my soul mate. All of these addictions wash through my insides and create a pool that never drains. My body is heavy with water: Swollen, floating. Mother dolphin snared in a fishing net.

* * *

Little boy, if circumstances were different, I might have had you. I might have weathered being sick for nine months straight. Risked the cyst bursting.

Son, I never wanted children. And I couldn't survive what my life had become and hold you above it.

I sit outside the apartment door on a warm winter desert night. Stars flood the southwestern sky. I see pieces of you float freely in this universal life of yours.

You race across clusters of constellations while my life stands still on Earth.

I'm afraid of your father, afraid of who you could have been, afraid of the shrinking amount of change in my jar.

Fourth Concussion

The metal bar with a loose wire is not at fault

Fat rash of pink spackled across cheeks 75 minutes afterwards

The five hundred dollar MRI says both hemispheres normal

To feel the outer perimeter of the brain squeeze itself

There is no medicine for light that goes sideways behind eyelids

I sit in the car with my credit card bill and discolored face

*   *   *

My mother's job at a London factory resulted in a concussion
Her auburn hair tangled in a machine that cut her head
She couldn't discuss the creek of blood or the bats that appeared on her street

Mother   We are here but untethered
Hover around a cliff's edge   like smoke that drifts
We are perpetual fog

*   *   *

I use the prefrontal cortex of my friend to interpret instructions for
getting divorced

I disappear behind the curtain of a warped winter and collapsed mood

Stitch myself to imaginary angels who offer wineskins filled with gin

I dream of a sixth sense that will carry my mind to the temple of the sun

Mermaid Overdose

1.
Your fluid-filled lungs leak
      into the lake of your chest.

Rivers swish inside your arms.

        That must be the reason for the
      elegance of your stroke. I'm with
each drop of you that flows
           into the Potomac. When you

    float by, I know that legs are tails, are tributaries.
    Everything about you

        leads to the sea and I can't get
    there as fast as my heart can fly.

2.
All those drugs disposed in the ocean:

You've absorbed them through your
      gills and pourous skin.

        Now you can't get enough of the high
    seas and I can't track you above or below

the water. Even when I toss an inner tube,
        you dive in the opposite direction.

Me wanting you to want to
             save yourself.

3.
        Watch me stand on the Maryland shore,
remembering your wet chest and

        pastel blue hands. You moved like a
                        ballerina. I sighed like a tired dog

                and drooled. How did your turquoise scales
become the body I loved?

4.
Imagine a trail of pills

across the sand. I bend over
                to pick one up.

One less for you to swallow,
        one more that might lead to your tail.

If only I could have entered your aortic chamber,
                healed the watery moon of your heart.

You were swimming
                through addiction
        and I had no say.

        Now I just listen for a beat,
a splash of you:

        Part woman, part fish,
                part unnamed star.

Pandemic Mercy

We seek mercy and not
grace
> —Gris Muñoz

We lived to ride the sun
like a carousel, never knowing
when we would fall off.

Tonight we seek solace in stars,
trust we'll see them despite the fog of illness
after the hospital turned you away.

I claw your chest open
to let moonlight into your lungs,
watch alveoli crawl across the stage
beneath your ribs.
It's still a beautiful show.

Hum to myself as I wait for you
to breathe a recognizable rhythm.

* * *

Melancholy the heat of fever
Melancholy the bark of the towering palm
Melancholy the souls who asked us to turn around hundreds of years ago.

* * *

This nation loves dollars,
ignores body counts.
We have slept with damage since our beginning.

The dead spin in the sky
fly above suffering, whisper don't refuse me now
after sun rips the horizon.

You create a gurgling sigh
and I know that even with hope in this kind of country,
we are on our own.

There are no working wings.
Just wandering for mercy.

Finding Costa Brava

Mother's liquid Dexedrine glows
Through the large glass bottle.

Cocoa tinted.

When she pours it into a tablespoon
It's a neon juice reveal:

Valencian orange glam syrup
Procured by dad that wakes her

From a narcoleptic haze.

In her orbit there are angel food cakes and
Pink Sno Balls

From the Hostess factory.
We binge on sugar to soothe.

She secretly smokes but I dig for the pack
In her purse, rip each cigarette

One by one, over the trash can
As father ordered.

I ruin her weight loss plan.

My birth chains her to him.
She drifts in and out of my life

Takes to her bed with migraines
And the opera of overwhelm.

Her sadness fills sinks and bathtubs.
I can't turn the faucets off.

She hides in the basement laundry room
Her bomb shelter from a second Blitz.

Father's belt whips recorded
By my blue arms and living room walls.

I open the hall closet, medicine filled,
Grab cherry red syrup with codeine.

The scenic Costa Brava wallpaper peels.
Yellow tiger's eye teeth fall out of my mouth.

For the Woman Who Knows Death and Loves Hard

You love hard
He says and then he leaves
I hear this and think yes—
Our bodies are 95 percent water
Gravity keeps me from floating away
I love hard
Facts I never question

I sex his body with subterranean touch
So much so that he cries in my embrace
And I hold him with the power of ten twisted arms
I am a village of love packed into one being
I love his tears his cock the backs of his legs
With my lips and this is too tender

He wants me intense when I'm next to his skin
When I listen with the loyalty of a Labrador
About every aching detail of his work
And two times he holds my grief
But the third time is one too many and it's too late
I am too much

I flood the streets of his desert town
Ask him to mop without meaning to
I still love my dead
They are like me—unbearable

He tells me 3 times *I have a fear of abandonment*
And then abandons me
I decide to love fire and burn incense every day
Nag champa to remember how I lit it when he came to visit
Copal to cleanse his being from my bed my closet
My olive green couch where he wooed me
Palo santo to give me back my home of loneliness

Burning incense 3 times a day is too much
I love fire hard
Put it out with tears
I hurricane my pain all over the floor I don't
Bother to mop it up
I would swallow that inconvenient grief if I could

You ocean of a woman, he says
I am tangled with seaweed
Love as if today were my last day on the planet
As if today were his last day here
I am greedy for his eyes that sing at night
And if he were to call tomorrow which he won't
I would know not to answer the phone

Gaslight Hair

From Puerto Rico to New York
After *Pariah* by Marcos Dimas, 1971-72

Your head a red glittering globe
surrounded by the steam of grief.

With a tumbling heart
you came to this grey-stained island,
saturated with people who rush.

Bulging sun ripens, rinses your hair
with a shroud of copper light,
even on a day like this.

This was the beginning of
life without enough shine,
solar bits still tailing you.

/

You stood on cobbled streets,
gaslight hair
with the unpredictable wave of the ocean.

And how you listened as if
my words were hibiscus petals
spilling from the mouth.

You look for a potion
to bring back who you used to be,
and take a sip as a wish for what's gone.

/

The bluegreen sea breathes with you
even as the chaos of this city
sprays a brown mist on your face.

You still inhale the days from our island years:
A lifetime of summer afternoons
when lust was a sculpture of chiseled embrace,

your tender face a page
in the book of the body
that reads love for centuries to come.

Potomac Ceremony

For M.S.

Your liquor, your pills
your razor, your blood
      that cold November afternoon

The radio played jazz in a hotel room
              beside the Potomac

    Gin bottle spilled where you last sang

Staggered from sink to flat beige carpet

           flapped your fleshy wings

    like a heron high off trumpet flowers

                from a summer backyard

    Take me home to my wife and kids
        I don't have to be gay

you begged on the note you left

           begged on the note

(and we wanted to tell you *yes you can* and
we love you more)

Revolving red lights

                        moon-stained streets

     pixelated stars

while you were unconscious in the ambulance

                your hearing the last to fade

/

This December day our bodies numb

     can't kiss your cheek before you leave

Your body now burned by flowered flames

       I keep some cinders   then smudge them

              on the heart of my black dress

We toss your ashes into the waves

                  watch them arabesque through winter air

Waiting On Lust for Life

The story goes like this:

                Death rearranges all the rooms.

Plants become crust.   Couch of crumbs.

           At night, vertebrae drifts into positions that won't hold.

/

When I wake the walls drip

               with lines of aqua dots.

If this is dissociation, I like it.
I plan on staying here

            in the places I can't understand.

Hypnotized by stillness.

          Waiting to raise the dead.

/

I see you sweat impatience.

It won't always be this way,
tendons frozen in my groin.

Can you hear me?

Someday I'll have sex again.

Ocean Time

The forceps that pulled me out of your womb

were stronger than my fetal resistance.

No one else could be as sick as you

with your menagerie of diseases.

My body became a watery house of prayer

to dispel illness. I fed myself blue bacteria for you.

Stored your buckets of sorrow under my tongue.

Stuffed my buckets of sorrow until I learned

to vomit the swell of sugar I ate.

Learned to evacuate my skeleton.

You: Slippery, sad, falling asleep at the wheel.

Me: Your 10-year-old copilot, waking you from narcolepsy and nihilation.

Made myself a refugee, moving state to state

living in Tucson, collecting a monsoon of medical debt.

I use baby wipes to clean my eyes. Get lost in tea leaves

that promise rescue if I can just hold on until June.

Mother, time is an ocean and the waves are slapping my thighs.

Blue Period

For Michael Hughes

Canvas of	blue	faces sprays the news
Of your death.		

You the	blue	flame.
Pilot light		of a thousand stoves.

Such	blue	-ness.
	Blue	streams overflow.
	Blue	skin with oxygen lost.
	Blue	heart too large for this room.

Hands	blue	from winter in the city you left.

Lungs		of cobalt
	blue.	
Voice of	blue	that shoos the clouds.

	Blue	bruises of life.
The biggest	blue	regret.

Empty	blue.	
Touchstone	blue.	

	Blue	veins stuffed with grief.
	Blue	lips pine to receive a kiss.

Twilight   blue.   Opiate
              blue.
Trip the   blue   fantastic.
              Blue   for too many miles.

Voyage blue   without you.

Second Concussion

Forgets to buckle seat belt

head smacks
                73 cracks

her mouth on the moon
howls

            drunk driver   leaves
metallic trail

Decade in the Dark: The Eighties

We enlist in the search for American heaven.
Silver glitter around our eyes,
all shimmer for a new wave face.

Time to slash and run from life.

Punks pointing out wars in
Nicaragua and El Salvador.

Black eyeliner, dark circles,
fingernails chewed.
Underground radio identity.
Sleeping pills have a paradoxical effect.
Pretend laughter, pewter clouds.

We hide in the hiding,
sing ghost machine songs.
Sheath of apartheid covers the globe.
Materialism sanctified.
The sky stays grey over the White House
the entire decade.

We are nomads who crawl across the city.
Black beauties and crack keep us awake
during HIV and homelessness.

Gay photographs censored.
The only flowers we see
in hospital rooms.

Everything captured in black and white.
Absence of sun ignored.

We dance in tunnels and tombs.
This darkness our iridescence.

Streetlights malfunction,
stars exit the celestial sphere.

We develop night vision
like wolves with nowhere to go.

Crawling Out

I tell myself I need a drink to deal with your kind.

The truth is never darker than the bluest night:

You stole luminaries from the sky until no one

could find their way home. I can no longer question

the safety of you.

What I mean is you had an astral hold on my arm,

kept telling me I was beautiful to brainwash my concussions,

steal my music in subtle ways.

Oh my familiar,
spacecharmer—

I created symbols and charts to crawl out of your cyclone.

This is unfinished: This discussion, this poem

about how I felt the vortex of all storms and

began to feel my skin again.

Our fathers watch from the end of the bar

while you promise to release the Eastern stars.

Heart With Legs

Close to the horizon is a boat
with a cargo of apologies.
The money is gone and all
that's left is the pigeon gray
we sailed away from.
The sun's overcast heat
makes your black curls sweat.
Someone said love is stronger
than a bank account
but the truth is frugal.
There was a covenant
to grow old together,
to travel the ocean of belief.
The begging I did to keep us
out of the red as we fell into the future.
Every blue wave hits the spine.
How driftwood branches decay
inside the brain, leaving pathways of disrepair.
How skin dries even in the damp salt air.
How heart grows legs and runs
in search of a fairy tale
where no one drowns.

In the Back Seat

Strap yourself in—this may be love lost or something like it.
We could go eons without touch, then a thought nicks the pineal gland.
That's how it is with us.
Suds build up in the kitchen sink and I telepath you.
You answer.
We're two creatures who became somewhat respectable.
But I'm floundering.

Let's meet in the middle of the country: A strange city that traces twilight.

I would claw out of my straitjacket for you.
I would fly to Pluto with you and leave these dishes behind.

My heart telegrams you.
My skin photocopies you.
I can't lie about love or the calendar. It says today is you.

Seahorses flock around me in the bathtub while I watch mindmovies of
our past.

I left the oven on. It bakes my heart at 375 degrees on a pan with sugar cookies.
Terrible sweetness.
Scent of your cheeks.

I'll wait for you in the back seat of my Toyota Corolla in this photo from 1989.

Esperanza en Andalucía

The moon stretches her legs and
kicks a bowl full of stars across the sky.

Each star drips the silver liquid of
salvation in Sevilla.

Passport to the Body's Country

I talk with dying dandelions after prayer
To fly away from my dislocated story

Let them offer white heads of wisdom
Before the breath of wind comes

I dance with milkweed at night
& hold the more of me when I can

Negotiate decades of despondence
Years without sisters

Recognize I stripped myself of cities
To find the right season

Carried love in caskets at each stop
& still no revelation

Brain cells blazed by jumps and falls
Into the next place

Devoured my body by the search
For ground that could be mine

Final destination: My bone marrow
I have the blood I need

These days I write my way into the light
Let go of lost maps

Remember I have earned a seat at the table of home.

IV

In the Dark Hours of the Owl

Raise your hands palm to palm:

      This healing power once dormant,
            swirling through odd-shaped clouds
for eons before landing
      transforms each of your hands into a torch of light.

Fingers filled with pomegranate seeds stacked inside each digit.
            Magic inherited from
                your malnourished grandmother
who read tea leaves to keep her children fed.

      You thought you were stagnant water
but your core is fire caught by wind.
            Your haunted heart runs into
sisters in need of regeneration
            in the dark hours of the owl.

Rub your seasoned hands together:

      Create circles in the air across sidewalks and centuries, then
            whisk a milk of white blood cells
                to transfuse into collapsing bodies.

            Reach for tired women curled in a cave
who speak in hieroglyphs, greedy for more than survival.
      For health instead of god.

No longer ghosts of their mothers, help them rise like divine trees—
each limb hissing courage in storms,
ready to strike lightning back to the sky.

Wartime World

Dear Paloma,
You are my nocturnal witness.
We were electric sparklers with dilated eyes
on the periphery of the Eastern horizon.
Drifting.

After we swam through the sky
I hitched a ride to Neptune,
found my family in caves:
Dead but shivering.
Killed by colossal crimes.

They never found heaven,
just kilometers of confusion.
Methane pools.

* * *

My clan blown away
but I hold explosions,
a waking dream of bodies.

Skin hangs from atrophied legs,
eyes blind from infrared suns.
Hearts outside of chests.

There is commotion in the psoas
that held femur and spine together.

Corpses hot and cold. Fever in the stratosphere.

Paloma, they are not anesthetized.

* * *

I didn't mean to land on this planet.
To see all this.

I don't know how to tell you about war,
how it splits open buildings and torsos.
Brains fall into purgatory, unable to sense the wind.
What kind of survival is that?

* * *

Paloma, I want to come home to you.
Let my body make a prayer out of holding yours.

I want to pick tulips for you.
Peruse thick photo albums and recall the flesh.
Forget the blood.

Remember how we were cigarettes always lit:
Young riots every night of the week,
celebrating supernovas without a map

dancing to music under guardian moons,
sucking on peace before our country cracked.

Growing Up Female Around American Shooters

To be female is to be raw 24/7.

Prodigal daughters with crooked haloes, oily hair

flesh full of open wounds that never close

because we are not desensitized:

We are only sharpened.

We wear helmets to protect our heads

from the low thunder of a coming stampede

that turns into gospel of guns:

Amateur killers coming for us.

We swing between tremors and sunlight—

Shaking under a desk or standing in a parking lot

where grackles pick at body bags.

Where is my body as we tread

between hustle and hallucinogenic?

We race to work fast food after school,

or run to huff spray paint in a rainbow of shades.

We're skilled at living in the ruins of our cities

despite nervous systems with the god blown out.

We are stars jumping earth to sky,

damned that we light the way for our dead.

I'm tired of drawing the blinds against muscular neon.

My throat is raw again.

Third Concussion

Coastal Georgia

Cardboard boxes pressed against wall at center of scene:

    Woman, 56, unpacks
    Man, 59, not home

She carries a box from bedroom
                          trips   falls

forehead smacks floor
            skull to tile

                   flames in the brain

         grey matter mud slide

she disappears under foundation   into dirt   merges with minerals

         travels to the top of the spinal cord

    walks a labyrinth of stars

becomes scavenger of sky that lands

      as vulture

                    picks at the rancid

        doesn't know how to stop

Sly & the Family Stone plays on a speaker:

                    "I Want to Take You Higher"

        lyrics spill from her scrounger head

a lump protrudes

she is confused

        what is pain   what isn't   please don't ask

memory loss renders her a Human What-Was-I-Just-Doing
                                        over and over

/

She longs to talk with the man

            who leaves work early, not getting paid

                ignores bills sent to collections for years

                        She thinks about smoking a cigarette
        after decades of abstaining

dreams of quasi-miracles to erase his loans

/

She wonders if hearts have concussions

unpacks another box
puts away forks

    considers what to do with the carving knife

        perhaps cut her chest

    use blood as river

        to enter the coastal waterway that leads to the sea

    better to drown there   than drown in debt

                She knows now

            she is no bird

            has no wings

                no chance at flight

Fire from the Longest Year

Let's ask gravediggers about grief

and the woman who turns on the crematorium fire.

Find the elder who lights

the funeral pyre in feral wind.

I stay awake with shadows

because there is no choice.

*

Ghosts beg me to talk

into the ethers out loud

since I'm exiled from a life with sugar.

Not that I need sugar

but wouldn't it be nice to indulge

a kid of calamities just once?

*

Weeping willow branches

have dried out enough to be

swallowed into flames that torch

bodies of our loved ones.

At what point do we call this many corpses immoral?

I want to torch myself.

*

Black smoke seeps into marrow of bereaved bones.

I fall into soil of the underworld

press my lips to the earth.

New Sun

For Francisco X. Alarcón
(Feb. 21, 1954 ~ Jan. 15, 2016)

We hear your voice
        in the western sky
                as firecracker snaps,
dance of comets,
                        Nahuatl chants.

We hear your voice   across groves of olive trees:
How it feeds green leaves, nourishes elder roots.

We hear your voice
        from coast to river to tributary
                      enter our veins,
vibrate as it circulates through slow-moving blood.

We hear your voice
like sagestick smoke that rises,
        becomes refuge from gunshots and police
                who target queer dark skin.

We hear your voice
                as a well-timed tremor of lightning
that invites lost sleepwalkers
                back to life.

We hear your voice
        at the border wall as it blooms into a lake of fire,
blaze of justice manifest
            under fierce maternal moon.

We hear your voice   invoke the four directions,
         migrate through the Milky Way, erupt
              as cosmic prayer, release
                    your marigold sun.

Open Letter to My Outer Space Lover

Intelligent Starman
Who Penetrates My Heart:
You are more than a trance.
You slide down
Like a piece of jade
From five centuries ago.
While the planets race,
You talk about love
& electric skies.
Take your traveling palms
& bless my trepidation.
Then move your hands
Across my open rose,
Make petals rise to
Your lighthouse in the sky.
Watch while I vibrate
From your nitrous oxide.
When I suck your raygun,
You squeeze rings
Around my moon.
I melt, then give birth
To a sizzling star.
This is galaxy fever.
There's a depth
To your heavenly body.
You're five thousand years
Of passion in this place
Where dizziness lives.

We don't need ground control
Or a spaceship with wheels.
Our adoration & the songs we sing
Live in the lusty clouds.

Mother's Hips

In the dream someone keeps repeating
that my mother is dead.

I keep saying no, she is of the frozen people
who can't recover from never being safe.

My mother looks at me as though she isn't here,
stares at an invisible constellation.

In the dream I prop her up against the wall,
teach her to give birth to the north node.

* * *

In the dream she is slumped over the toilet,
ambulance siren closing in, another Valium overdose.

In the dream I tell her my name four times,
wait for her to say my name *please say my name.*

In the dream my mother's pelvis murmurs in blue.
It tilts toward the hinge of shivering.

In the dream she fades under a male corpse.
She doesn't say *I can't speak* but I hear her.

* * *

In the dream the cat we named Nina appears.
Her onyx fur reflects flying stars.

In the dream Nina is warm to the touch.
Mother's eyes the color of milk.

Red Dirt Road

After internal bleeding took my father
I released the air out of my ego,

became a deflated balloon in the bed of my life.

Friends who couldn't understand brokenness
backed away. I was contagious with grief

that turned yellow in a Petri dish.

At night the moon turned toward my face,
forced me to peel off the self-hatred I wore

under long sleeves of a black shirt I never washed.

I tore down the fence that penned me in
to a backyard of sadness and snow.

Dropped beloved books to discharge weight, flee across state lines.

When daylight came, I shook off infection:
White blood cells gathered to conquer disease.

The horizon showed itself and I knelt in the wind.

Refugees with hellish dreams approached the red dirt road.
I was a whirling top under the sun.

My arms opened to wave them in, to welcome all the beings of the broken world.

Acknowledgments

Many thanks to the editors of the following journals and anthologies for publishing the following poems and prose, sometimes in earlier versions:

- *Anti-Heroin Chic*: "Finding Costa Brava," "Godmother"
- *The Banyan Review*: "Mermaid Overdose" and "Watching the War, 1975"
- *Black Earth Institute*: "Pandemic Mercy"
- *Boundless 2023: The Anthology of the Rio Grande Valley International Poetry Festival*: "Walls"
- *Eleven Eleven*: "Blue Period"
- *Headline Poetry & Press*: "Pandemic Mercy"
- *IMANIMAN: Poets Writing in the Anzaldúan Borderlands*: "Water Bottles at the Border"
- *The Manifest-Station*: "Boy With No Name"
- *Origins Literary Journal*: "Refugee Couple"
- *OyeDrum Magazine*: "For the Woman Who Knows Death and Loves Hard," "Swollen Heart"
- *Poet Lore*: "Gaslight Hair"
- *Rogue Agent*: "Post-War Hunger," originally published as "Hunger Dream"
- *Soñadores: We Came to Dream*: "New Sun"
- *Tahoma Literary Review*: "Mother's Hips"

Gratitude

To my editor jo reyes-boitel, whose expert advice and emotional support helped shaped this book: Thank you.

To ire'ne lara silva, thank you for your deeply thoughtful introduction and unconditional support.

To Francisco Aragón, the director of Letras Latinas, thank you for giving me the opportunity to collaborate with you and your stellar Latinx literary initiative.

Thank you for your generous endorsements of this book: Sheila Black, John Olivares Espinoza, Angelina Sáenz and Pamela Uschuk.

To Aydee Lopez Martinez, thank you for sharing your powerful art to grace the cover.

To FlowerSong Press publisher and poet Edward Vidaurre, thank you for bringing me into the FlowerSong family.

To the San Antonio poetry community, thank you for welcoming me with open arms.

About the Author

Carmen Calatayud is the daughter of immigrants: A Spanish father and Irish mother. Her book *In the Company of Spirits*, published by Press 53, was a runner-up for the Academy of American Poets Walt Whitman Award and a finalist for the Andrés Montoya Poetry Prize. Her work has appeared in journals such as *Anti-Heroin Chic, Cutthroat, Gargoyle, OyeDrum, Poet Lore, Rogue Agent, Tahoma Literary Review* and *Verse Daily,* and in numerous anthologies. She is a Larry Neal Poetry Award winner, a Best of *La Bloga* winner and a Virginia Center for the Creative Arts fellow. She lives in San Antonio, Texas.

About the Artist

Aydee Lopez Martinez is a painter and ceramic artist based in Covina, California. She has a bachelor's degree in fine art from California State University-Los Angeles. Her work has been shown throughout California, in Arizona, and in New York, Chicago and Juarez, Mexico. In addition to painting and ceramics, she creates works with mosaic glass and natural stones. She has illustrated several children's books, and her work appears on the covers of several poetry and short story books. Visit aydeeart.com.

FLOWERSONG
PRESS

**FlowerSong Press nurtures essential verse
from, about, and throughout the borderlands.
Literary. Lyrical. Boundless.**

Sign up for announcements about
new and upcoming titles at:

www.flowersongpress.com

www.ingramcontent.com/pod-product-compliance
Lightning Source LLC
Chambersburg PA
CBHW031445120626
46545CB00006B/2557